CICERO
THE
QUEEN'S DRUM HORSE

by James Drummond · illustrated by Elisabeth Grant

 Holmes McDougall Limited, Edinburgh.

Author: James Drummond.
Illustrator: Elisabeth Grant.
Printer: Holmes McDougall Ltd., Aberdeen.
Publisher: Holmes McDougall Ltd., 30 Royal Terrace, Edinburgh.
Copyright © Holmes McDougall Ltd., 1972.

ISBN: 7157 1024–9

Mr. and Mrs. O'Kelly and their five children lived in a small farmhouse on the slopes of the Mountains of Mourne in Ireland. One morning Mr. O'Kelly came in with the exciting news that Shona the chestnut mare had just had a foal.

The children wanted to rush off to see the foal straight away but Mrs. O'Kelly said that they must eat their breakfast first. "Foal or no foal," she declared, "I won't have good food wasted in this house."

Maureen was the first to finish. "Oh look!" she said.

"You can see the foal from here. He's having his breakfast too. Hurry up and we'll all go up together."

The children knew not to frighten the new-born foal or worry his mother by going too close to him. As the days went by the little foal became less timid. He would come to meet them when they stood at the gate.

"We must find a new name for the foal," said Mrs. O'Kelly. All the five children thought very hard. "Soldier," suggested Michael, "because he is such a brave little foal."

"Samson," said Maureen, "because he is so strong."

"I think Patch is a good name," said Eileen. But none of the names seemed just right.

As usual it was Mrs. O'Kelly who got them out of their difficulty. "I know," said Mrs. O'Kelly, at last. "He was born on St. Patrick's Day, so why not call him Paddy?" Everybody at once agreed that Paddy was the only possible name for him. It had a nice friendly sound. And he certainly was a friendly horse, always willing to join in the children's games, even the noisy ones.

When Paddy was two years old Mr. O'Kelly said that he was strong enough to carry somebody on his back. So the children decided to have a grand procession to celebrate St. Patrick's Day and Paddy's second birthday.

And it really *was* a grand procession because by this time there were more O'Kelly's than there had been when Paddy was born.

Processions soon became a favourite game with the
O'Kelly family. There were no real trumpets or drums on
the farm, but there were things like an empty biscuit tin
to whack with a spoon, pot lids to bang together and
rolls of cardboard that gave a booming sound when
you shouted through them.

Paddy loved it.

Very soon, when he heard the rat-a-tat-tat of a biscuit tin drum he would prick up his ears and twitch his nose with excitement as he trotted down the field to join the procession.

At last the time came when Paddy was old enough
to work, so Mr. O'Kelly took him to the horse market.
Maureen was allowed to go too.

The children were sorry to see Paddy go, but they
knew it was time he started to earn his living.

There were all sorts of animals for sale at the market.
What a busy place it was! Some of the animals were
frightened by the noise, but Paddy enjoyed the bustle
and excitement. Anyway he felt quite safe with Mr.
O'Kelly and Maureen by his side.

A man called Mr. Stuart came up and looked at
Paddy. He had come from Scotland to find a good
working horse.

There were certainly plenty of horses to choose from. First he looked at a grey mare, but he quickly decided not to buy *that* one. He patted the chestnut's nose and gave him a lump of sugar, but he didn't seem to think he would do at all. And anybody who knows anything about horses would know that the black horse was a thoroughly bad-tempered animal.

But Mr. Stuart liked Paddy as soon as he saw him. After he had spoken to Mr. O'Kelly for quite a long time he gave him some money and led Paddy away. Very soon Paddy and his new master were in a big boat on their way to Scotland.

After a long journey and many adventures Paddy arrived in Edinburgh. He was put to work as a milk horse pulling a milk cart for St. Cuthbert Co-operative Society.

Paddy was put in the care of one of the best milkmen, Willie Wilson. Every morning Willie Wilson would harness Paddy to his milk cart.

While Willie Wilson was doing this the boy who helped him would be busy loading hundreds of bottles of milk onto the milk cart. The boy's name was Jock. Then the three of them would set off on their rounds taking the milk to people's houses in time for breakfast.

The sign above the entrance to the dairy shows that this is where the Queen gets her milk when she stays in the Palace of Holyroodhouse, in Edinburgh. The Palace is not far from the dairy.

Paddy soon found that it was hard work being a milk horse. During the first few weeks his back was often sore and his legs ached with pulling the heavy cart. When Willie Wilson saw that Paddy was getting tired he would say "Gee up, Paddy old boy. We'll soon be home and then I'll give you a nice feed of oats while Jock here gives the cart a good polish." And Jock would whistle a tune to cheer him up. Paddy soon became very fond of his two new friends. Like Mr. O'Kelly and Maureen they knew how important it is to speak to horses, even if they don't understand every single word that is being said.

As the weeks went by Paddy's legs grew stronger
and his back didn't ache any more. He began to enjoy
being a milk horse. Because he was so good-natured
he made lots of friends as he stood patiently in the
street while Jock and Willie Wilson ran up and down
steps delivering the milk.

His new friends were so kind to him that sometimes
Willie Wilson had to say "Please don't give Paddy any
more carrots or sweets or he'll be too fat to do his work."
He liked the busy streets and all the exciting noises
—the roar of the traffic, the happy jingle of his harness
and the nice clattering noise the milk crates made as his
cart rattled over the cobbled streets. And, of course,
Jock's cheerful whistle.

There is a famous street in Edinburgh called The Royal Mile. It got its name because it runs between Edinburgh Castle and the Palace of Holyroodhouse. One day when they came to the Royal Mile, Willie Wilson pulled on the reins. "Woa there Paddy! Here come the soldiers. We'll have to stop to let the procession go by".

Willie Wilson thought that Paddy had never heard a band before, so he said to Jock "Quick, Jock! Jump down and hold Paddy's reins in case he is frightened by the noise of the drums."

But he needn't have worried. Paddy wasn't a bit frightened by the roll of the drums and the skirl of the bagpipes. As the procession approached he pricked up his ears and twitched his nose as if to say "I like most noises, but of all the noises I really like, the noise of a band is the best."

After the band came a big black car with a flag on its bonnet. Everybody waved and cheered as it passed. This time it was Willie Wilson who was excited. "That was the Queen, Jock! And did you see the way she turned and looked straight at Paddy?"

"Och don't be silly" said Jock. "Why would the Queen want to look at a milk horse? It must have been my nice shiny cart she took a fancy to."

But Willie Wilson was right. It was the horse, not the cart, that the Queen had taken a fancy to. Not long after this a message came to the dairy that the Queen wanted to see the milk horse that did the Royal Mile milk round. That was Paddy.

Willie Wilson and Jock were very excited. They groomed Paddy. They brushed his coat till it was sleek and shining.

The next day they took Paddy to the Palace. A crowd of important looking people stood in the stable yard looking him up and down. Among them was the Queen. Paddy began to feel nervous. Then the Queen came up and stroked his neck and spoke to him. Suddenly Paddy was not afraid any more. He twitched his ears and put down his head, as if to say "Here is somebody *else* who knows how to speak to a horse."

The Queen was certainly very interested in Paddy. She wanted to see him walk and trot. She asked one of the soldiers to measure him and another to look at his teeth. She wondered if he had sturdy muscles and if he had a strong back. The inspection lasted a long time.

Finally the Queen examined his eyes and said "Yes. He is intelligent and good natured. He will do splendidly". Then she patted his nose. "I think that we will call him Cicero" she added, and then went back into her palace.

The next day Willie Wilson and Jock took twice as long as usual to do their milk round. Another horse was pulling the milk cart. "Where has Paddy gone?" asked the customers.

Willie Wilson smiled proudly. "The Queen has bought him and he'll be on his way to London now," he said. Everyone started asking questions. "The Queen! Paddy is going to be a royal horse?" "What kind of work is he going to do?" Willie Wilson seemed a little sad. He was going to miss his horse.

Jock pretended not to care, but he didn't whistle for a week after Paddy went off to London.

Paddy—or Cicero, which was the new name the Queen had given him—was quite happy. He was put in a stable beside a lot of other horses. The stable seemed to belong to soldiers. Everything was very bright and smart and exciting. The Captain told a soldier called Trooper Hutsby to look after the new horse, and he did it very well.

In the next box to Cicero was a big horse called
Hector. Very soon the two horses were the best of
friends.

Cicero and Hector seemed to be the only brown and white horses in the stables. The other horses belonged to the soldiers whose job it was to guard one of the entrances to Buckingham Palace.

Trooper Hutsby spent hours each day grooming his horse. Cicero liked best when he had his coat cleaned with the vacuum cleaner. He liked the noise and tickly feeling. Soon his coat gleamed and his hooves shone like glass. "Now, Cicero my boy," said Trooper Hutsby, "you've a lot to learn before you can work for the Queen, but you just watch Hector here and do what he does, and you can't go wrong."

It took many months to train Cicero for his new job.
Trooper Hutsby was kind and patient, but he made
Cicero work hard.

"Head up now, Cicero," Trooper Hutsby would say.
"Don't forget that when you are ready for work there
will be thousands of people watching you."

Cicero had to learn to turn left or right at the same
time as the other horses. It helped a lot to have
Hector at his side.

"Stand out now, Cicero! Feet planted wide apart.
You'll have to stand quite still for hours, with a heavy
load on that strong back of yours." Trooper Hutsby
was surprised and delighted at how well Cicero did this.
Even Hector couldn't do it any better than Cicero.
When Cicero pulled the milk cart in Edinburgh he had
had plenty of practice in standing still while Jock went
to the customers' houses.

One morning as Cicero was being led out to the parade ground he heard a sound that made him prick up his ears and twitch his nose.

It was the sound of drums, and who should be
carrying them but his friend Hector! What a splendid
job for a horse! And when Trooper Hutsby saw that
Cicero wasn't a bit frightened by the noise he was
delighted. "I tell you what, Cicero," he said, "It looks to
me as if we could have you ready for work quite soon.
Then the Life Guards will have *two* drum-horses—you
and Hector."

A drum-horse! So *that* was why he had been brought all the way to Buckingham Palace!

The first time Cicero got the drum on his back he was so happy he tossed his head and pawed the ground. *"Don't* do that," said Trooper Hutsby. "Now that you are a drum-horse in the Queen's band you must remember to stand still even when you are doing exciting things."

Of course Cicero still had weeks and weeks of practice to go through before he was ready to take part in a big procession.

But at last the day arrived, and a very special day it was—it was the Queen's birthday!

Thousands of people had come to see the Queen
ride down from Buckingham Palace to the Horse
Guards Parade to inspect her soldiers.

And at the very front of the procession came
Cicero the Drum-Horse.

Trooper Hutsby was thumping away at two of the
most beautiful silver drums you have ever seen. They
were decorated with the sign that showed they belonged
to the Queen.

Everybody who saw the procession thought that Cicero did splendidly, but there were three people who were specially pleased with him.

Trooper Hutsby was delighted that Cicero remembered to stand to attention as a soldier's horse should.

And there was a man in the crowd who had come all the way from Edinburgh to see his old friend. He was so glad to see that, although Cicero the Drum-Horse was much smarter than Paddy the Milk-Horse had ever been, he hadn't really changed and was still as happy and friendly as ever. That, of course, was Willie Wilson.

And there was a third person who was particularly
proud of her new Drum-Horse. But you don't need to be
told who *she* was.